CW00525226

Waiting Spaces:
a poetry collection

Foreword by Dr. Sean Wiebe

Acacia Mitchell

Stunning writing with incredible precision and remarkable insight.

-Mark Daley, English teacher at *Heritage Christian Online School*

First time that I've read so much poetry...I finally understand why people like it.

- R.M Scheller, Freelance Editor, *rmscheller.com*

This book is for everyone and anyone who seeks to make sense of themselves, the world and others.

-John Caldwell, author of *'The Lion's Roar'* and *'Christ, the Cross and the Concrete Jungle'*

This is a book you simply cannot miss. Relatable, poignant and written by an incredibly talented young woman.

-Abbie McNutt, writer at *Tinkering Feathers, tinkeringwithfeathers.home.blog*

Acacia's poetry immersed me in emotion and memories, and left me feeling understood and connected.

-Maya Joelle, writer at *The Stories are True, mayajt.wordpress.com*

Certain poems have been previously published on Thoughts From a Tree, the author's blog.

Illustrations by Sophie Torrance and used with permission.

Cover Designer: Zakarianada

ISBN: 9798652231781

To my parents, for loving me despite myself and always
letting me try.

To family and friends who have championed me
as I wrote this.

To Mr. Daley, who made me think that I could.

To God, all glory.

Table of Contents

Chapter Five

The healing

Foreword

Some who speak into our lives set us on fire: We hear a call; we cast our nets on the other side of the boat. In *Waiting Spaces*, I hear the voice of the young philosopher in conversation with her maker. Mitchell uses the site of her own life as the source to question the existential human assumptions that can keep the heart closed.

In this collection you will find a vulnerable soul setting out to understand being and belonging, adventure and home, time and timelessness.

For all of those who want to live their lives beyond the frames of reference that confine human thinking, Mitchell reminds us that our wildness is not a design flaw, but exactly who and where we are meant to be.

~Dr. Sean Wiebe, author of *How Boys Grow Up*, *Blue Waiting*, and *The Poet and the Pea*.

P r e f a c e

I have often wondered why God makes us wait for things.
I'm very impatient. I want to understand *now*. I want to
experience everything *now*. Buy the thing, eat the cake, form
the friendship without needing to try so hard.

But when I step back and watch what God has done in the
waiting, it blows away all of my doubts.

The waiting spaces are places that God uses to redeem us, to
help us focus on him and choose to give him glory.

Many of these poems were written as letters to dear friends.
Some were written to myself, from the perspective of God,
Abba, trying to teach me.

Above all, I hope these poems help you through your own
waiting spaces, to see Jesus in those places.

He's waiting there for us to turn to him.

One

the longing for belonging

To the place I visited and where my heart stayed

I miss the hot humid evenings of
walking and no fear and
laughter over everything.
You taught me to accept acceptance and to
reject rejection.
It's a rare thing to find
people who are of the same mind and
who set you on fire more
than you were before they were in your life.
But eventually,
you have to leave.
They leave, you leave
and as you realize this
your soul starts to grieve.
Your heart weaves
fantasies and melodies and
half-true stories of what might have been…
because let's face it.
It's easier to dream than to
live in the moment.
It's painfully easy to lose your focus.
It's hard to remember that
life is formed of
the small sidewalk cracks that take you back to
when you were two or

the familiar people who become so routine that it seems as
though they are no longer needed.
Patterns repeated over and over lose
the colour that you used to see.
Don't let them.
Let the repetition be
a part of the dance
and still
when it seems to cage you in and the stage you're in gives
no room to breathe
allow your soul to break free.
Life was not made to stay the same,
from day to day,
from place to place.
But we forget to be brave.
You, you are allowed to make waves
right where you are.
Don't aim for the stars, they'll only burn you, and
words said in secret will stay and hurt you.
Don't let them.

Breathe deep and release
the memories and you will see
this place can be made into paradise.

To the one choosing to worship in darkness

i thought that
twilight came slowly, softly
small twinkling lights appearing,
searing blaze
silhouette standing, unfazed
and i supposed that, with twisted irony,
i

        was

                  right.
the only thing i had failed to notice is that
the twilight had crept up
before my sight had let it sink into my mind that
the light had dimmed and the day had
d

  i

    e

      d.
help me find my bearings; You're
tearing me in different directions, one
that craves the brightness of day and one that seeks solace in
the stars.
at Your discretion our paths are made so who
am i
to tell You that this light shouldn't fade?
please,
as i dread this coming darkness
teach me to rejoice in new seasons of starlight.

To menial things

New leaves
(breathe deep)
Blended and yet
easily seen.
Life givers and
common weeds.
Do not despise the menial things.

To cherished places and new seasons

Bittersweet
sunset meets
the horizon and I realize
it's time to move away.

Sunsets fade and so do memories
revisiting this place means remembering
not only the things that I wish I could forget but also
letting myself see the good.

I'm not sure which hurts worse
never seeing beauty or never forgetting it
never letting it wash over your soul and ease your tired mind
or
lying awake every night
wishing that you could go back.

They say that everything comes in time but the longer that
you watch a sunset
the more its colours subtly blend and bend and
mend themselves from
one seamless skyline to another.
Soon you can't tell them apart from each other.
It's gone and we say
that this explosion of colour
has become less.

Less entrancing, more mess. Something that takes more steps
to find the allure and the
peace and the
rest.

Why do we expect big experiences to be the most gratifying?

Maybe
as this sunset fades
from beauty and fire to the end of the day
you'll find
in deep hues of blue and small specks of light
it's bittersweet for old days to dim
but this time of night
has its own glory.

To the one who needs rest

I'm trying
late at night
to listen to the sound of quiet. Of silence.

Let your shoulders fall and relax your jaw.
Don't be afraid if today you see nothing at all that makes
you proud to say "I did that, I achieved that, I fought for that
because I believe that."
Relish in that your heart is still beating, lungs expand and
you're still breathing,
mind rests, worries fleeing
forget them all and
begin sleeping.

To the one who regrets

Yes, there are times when you could have tried
or done
or said
or pulled the line
of a different thread
but these things do not define you.
Set all these worries behind you.

To the one unsure of where to call home

Home is running barefoot through a forest path, yelling all
the way in case there are bears.
There never are, but we enjoy the rush.

Home is calling friends at unnatural times because time
zones don't care who's missing who.

Home is my grandma's perfume seeping through the scarves
she's left behind, heartache to feel her touch like I feel the
fabric I'm fingering and, oh God, why is everyone so far
away?

Home is yelps and screams because someone just lost a nerf
war and SOMEONE is going to pay for it.

Home is the stinging wind on my skin as I half-stumble
down a loch's shore, processing, listening, unsure.

Home is salt in my mouth and my ears and chills all up my
body and smiles on my face because yes,
we jumped in again and no,
we weren't supposed to.

Home is watching the ground rise up towards you as the
plane falls.

Home is my mother's soft voice telling me to calm down,
late night chats with my dad

disorganized card games with my brothers and cries of "you cheated AGAIN".

Home is people together, lifting their voices, one purpose, Abba we worship you.

Home is a journey.

To the one who feels distracted

listening to you, abba
is like staring at the stars.
you can only see them shine bright
when you walk away from the other, closer lights
the ones that cloud your view and dim your sight.
nothing changes overnight.
stars will set and sun will rise and i may not have rested my eyes
but
slowly, over time, i have learned.
i am learning.

Two

the dissatisfaction

To the one who feels small

It's hard to wait. It's hard when everyone else's pace
seems to go more or bloom faster or
feel the warmth of the sun more than your corner of the
earth.
Sometimes I sit and wonder why the sky seems to heap
blessings on some and
forget others.
Perhaps it's to remind us to care for each other.

To the people I met but don't know

Count them on your fingers
places, streets.
Count them on your toes
faces, people.
A cacophony of colour and sounds and voices,
too many to be counted and too many to each be
permanent.

Just go with it.
Same stories, same conversations
same tones and gestures, slight
variations on the ones before it.
Abhorrent.
Ignore it.
I'm ignoring the
polite conversations with polite answers, the bored stares,
the
cough-coated attempts to cover up the space, the silence
while these swiftly moving figures invade my mind and pull
me away and I wonder about
her face, his face
what place are
they in now, wonder if I could trace
them back and revive
relive, rewrite
the lives where we all thrived together.

Open up my mind's eye and
tomorrow
I make more polite conversations.

To the one who wants tea

i'm going to boil the kettle, want some
tea and a good chat?
you could tell me anything in the time it takes to boil this
kettle-
did i
ever mention my first move?
it was fast and violent and new and still it
is summed up before this kettle has even reached a murmur.
you, you said earlier that
you'd just broken up with your boyfriend?
tell me, how are you? let me listen. what kind of tea do you
want again?
so who are you now? how do you see yourself?
yes, you are so beautiful.
yes, this is supposed to hurt.
you felt known and like you'd conquered the earth
to fall from that height will always turn
your world upside down.
here's my shoulder, lean on it. you'll get through. i'm here
for you.

did i ever tell you
how my grandfather died of cancer?
it was so painful
and so slow,
slower than this kettle boiling and yet it seems as if he died
so much faster that it is ready.

he liked tea- do you want milk?- and he painted. so
beautifully.

here, the kettle is done and please
tell me more.

To the ones who are gentle

flighty bird, mocked for their sensitivities and subtly
we
try to draw them closer
just to prove that we can
and yet, when people trust too much and get hurt
and find that humanity is worse
than their innocence would lead them to believe
we chide and say that they were naïve to
jump so far, fly so fast
caution is mocked but
recklessness can't last.

To those in unjust situations that I will never fully be able to understand

One, two, afternoon
cherry blossom tree
now I have to forfeit your solitary safety
bird-singing silence and
everlasting green.

Out of sight, out of mind
scared of unheard screams.
I don't deserve to live in a world
where everything is free.
It's unjust for you to wallow in fear
while I do as I please.

One, two, thirteen
petals fall from your dreams
place of peace, holy refrain
refrain me from my return again.

To the one who feels unseen: empathy

I went off in an attempt to locate value for myself in other
people's hands.
Watch me dance in robotic rhythm to your song
or don't watch, after all,
you can't see me.
I am gone.

To the one fighting anxiety

Hands are shaking and somehow, after years of practice
I've forgotten how to breathe.
Two twin birds are chasing each other around my belly, one
is called excitement and she is rose-gold-two-tone
can't-stand-to-be-alone-feathers-round-her-dreams.
The other,
his name is doubt and he is the colour of the sea at storm,
not the same shade for a second, constantly
changing and moving and trying to escape.
The two are so alike that
were you colour blind
you could not tell them apart but I can hear them
singing from my belly
sweet sense of time undone as the two
lose track of time and
excitement is trying to stop doubt from fleeing,
from molting his wings and ceasing to fly.

She wins.

To the one who has no time

Time
is an ice cube in the cup of your palm
if you savour it, let it land in the soft parts of your hands
observe its delicate intricacies, the mysteries
wait for each bubble to come to the top and marvel as each
small stream of water finds each canal in
your skin and wanders in imperfect lines
it lasts.
It winds its way into seconds and minutes and hours and
days and yet
if the ice cube is squeezed
pushed into place
held onto in an attempt to make it stay
it falls far faster through the cracks in your fist.
Ice turns to water and water to decisions made out of haste,
and a waste of hours and minutes, time
time is a river rushing full force, bank overflow, unsure of its
course and to
stand up and wade would swallow you with remorse, you
see
time is an ice cube and if you hold it too tight
you'll create the very thing that you're trying to fight and
hours and minutes will fall from the ice.

To loneliness

It's a helpless feeling.
It's a feeling that she can't manage
a feeling that others cannot manage her and
that when she tries to reach out for help
everyone will get hurt.

To twelve-year-old Acacia, moving

Ten, four,
fifteen
cherry blossoms
pristine
I watch the green alive around me
Where am I? Where am I?
Cross my heart and hope I fly
ignore my heart and wish for death.
Cold air, piercing deep, please
let me catch my breath.

Little bird, cherry tree
you know where to find safety
one grows intertwined in the arms of another
twigs fall, birds find
soon you'll be a mother.
Do you find, cherry tree, that it's hard to bear
the weight of life that grows inside and

Twenty-two, twenty-three
petals fall carelessly
bare to buds to blossoms to bare
take care, take care.
Little bird, find another home
even though it will go
before you know you're there.

Green to brown and brown to dreams
strange how we treasure short-term things.

To grief

I am in a glass box
and I don't know how to escape it.

I have seen tigers ablaze and
actors fake it, half wrung clothes
spread out to dry knowing
no one would come to take them in because
their purpose had been washed away like the dirt that stained
them.

I see colours become grief in the sink that is my belly,
constantly filling and draining and bubbling with every new
emotion but
so rarely empty and quiet and calm.

I have felt the grind and the crunch, the smooth sweet
friction of glass,
brittle and metallic and clear, shard and crack and finally
snap bang broken
flood held behind blockage beneath, breeze
kept out come rushing in for it is no longer a breeze
but a gale ready to strip out the remaining brokenness.

Tomorrow, don't forget me. Don't forget the glass I was now
that I am real.

To the one who feels incomplete and unseen

No longer am I restrained to these simple phrases
open up and
inside are faces
things existing only in the pictures others see me as.
Which is the real face?
Spare me from these faces I'm imprisoned to, colour me
deep hues. Deep red, deep blue
love is a purple colour.

It's made from blood and tears and royalty
hopes and fears and loyalty
laughter in deepest dark and honesty in brightest light.
Alas, we see through a dimmed window
into unknown realms of grace.

Three

the resting

To the one who must surrender

and in the oppressive presence of silence
when your heart is wild and
when the choices at hand demand more than you can give
remind yourself that you cannot be enough
but He is enough for you.

To the broken one, slowly finding grace

Shame is no longer a way of life.
It's gone.
I took that.
You are now my bride.
The lie that says "you are unloved" has been stripped away,
unwrapped, undone, rewritten by grace,
gone from the light because light wins over darkness and
soft wins over hardness and
all this is inconsistent with your former lens.
Remember when you first felt my love and remember how
you questioned if it would ever be enough and
I am.
Oh child, I am.

To the one who feels broken

It's only a matter of time
before the light shines through and you find
that what He said was true all along.
You are new.

To the one in a difficult place

in the morning you can awake knowing that
though circumstances haven't changed
neither has the fight inside you.

To the one who is misunderstood

but daughter
how they live does not define you
release the life that dances inside you
let yourself love regardless of the way it's received,
perceived, or believed in.
let yourself wrestle through questions until you have
answers that satisfy and
until what you do gratifies and
until your confidence rises high and you no longer have to
strive because
you are already more than worthy.
You are more than worthy.

To death: unvictorious

every petal will eventually fall from the flower from whence
it came.
but even after its full glory is depleted those petals can be
arranged, formed and shaped into something different.

with it comes new value. a new goal.
a new making of the old rose into something which is not
just seen and smelt but felt to contribute something else.

To the burned out one

breathe in
exhale
rewind
take the time
to fail
don't get caught up in
boxes and lines and tickets and fines and this,
this defines me and I can't move past and I can't remember
when my soul last
rested.
instead, take the time to laugh
to stop
to break
to slow down and appreciate
the season that you're in today

yesterday was a gold-tinted rose
thorns speckled the stem but in the end,
something beautiful became of it
something beautiful was made of it

and today is a new start;
letting go of this dying rose for one that hasn't yet bloomed.

leave room for silence. leave room for growth.
leave room for days when you are tired and you simply
cannot go.

learn to embrace this place even in the face of continually
walking alone.
learn to see yourself as you are, free of scars and people-
pleasing and
disbelief in all your dreaming.

embrace today and soon
tomorrow will bloom.

To the one who feels exhausted

we're afraid of judgment. afraid of failing.
afraid of cutting back in case it's seen as bailing
afraid of admitting what burdens we carry in case
others become wary and shun us away.
and in the midst of all of this, He comes into our shame
into the rejection and into the pain
into the places we want to erase and He sees.
sees it all and says that we are still welcome at His table.
we are still welcome
at His table.

To my beloved

For I will call the one who is not loved
                                    beloved.
                                    remade.
There is no cause for disdain.
Now, from this day
you
                    are
                                    saved.
Child of the living God, you who saw
pain like no one could believe, I not only saw but I
redeem
and now you are beloved.

To the one who doesn't feel beautiful

Look in the mirror
analyze every feature
even though neither
they nor the mirror actually tell me who I am.
I still trust them, lust after everything they say that I can
gain from this pain.
Suck in, breathe small
don't slouch, stand tall
one more mile before I fall. One more mile
before
I
fall.

Is this all? Is this all?
The reflection that I reflect on isn't the same one that you
see.
"This is me. This is me."

Scars and stretch marks stretch my ideas of how hard I can
push.
"This is me. This is me."

They've never glanced my way but I'm scared in case they
take a second look.
"This is me. This is me."

So instead,
let's get rid of that double chin,
smile wide, pull in the loose skin,
don't let hunger win. Don't let   hunger   w i n.
Stay fit, get thin.
Forget who I am within. Forget who I am within.

"Listen," you said,
"beauty comes from the inside."
But beauty is an overrated word, one that I've heard too
many times for it to mean anything to me.
So I smile and nod and try to hide
the lies, the lies   the   lies   t h e   l i e s
I forget who I am inside.
I forget that You cry every time. Every time.
Will I let me
try?

Can I
realize that I cannot see
the reflection and be satisfied
unless I first see through your eyes?

Perfect, fallen, broken, loved.
This is me. This is me.

To the one whose plans have changed

the tomorrow that you dreamed of
has faded and
changed but its loss has aided you, and
out of the ashes the light is making
something new
something more true than anything you've known before.

To Abba

faithful one, so unchanging.
morning sun, holding by me.

To the one who needs to remember

Remember
"And it came to pass."
This storm, this darkness
will not last.
This storm, this darkness
cannot last.

Four

the searching

To the one who compares

often times
inadequacy
is not defined by how full my cup is
but how full theirs is.

please, overflow my cup and teach me that the spill is part
of the journey.

To the ones who don't fit

wild things, wild flowers
age old times and half an hour
repairs, returns,
simplistic answers.
daffodils or wild panthers.

we tell people to follow the system
sit down, shut up
fit it all in and fit in with it all.
and yet, in the places where we find unexpected life
the sidewalk cracks and the ocean tide
we document it.
replicate it.
praise it for its natural beauty.
perhaps we are secretly jealous because we ourselves cannot
see
the beauty that naturally etches itself into our own
wild places.

To the one seeking authenticity

This time of life is a constant swirl
one where you constantly analyze your world,
where choices are hurled too fast to blink
no space to think or
breathe in.

Maintaining appearance is draining
straining for answers is paining
constant go and no stop and
no listen and all talk and
never reaching past what you thought
about A-line dresses and blue shoes;
"What's new?"
"Not much!"
Don't want them to touch that one spot in case it
all falls out and leaves you doubting whether they even
wanted to know.
Go.
Embrace calm.
Maybe this dance and song has reached an ending and it's
time to move on.

Time to explore things that, before, had no meaning
to find old dreams and start dreaming because
this shallow existence will never gratify.
Never satisfy.

It will only leave you petrified that this is all you have to die
for.
To live for.
Pursue more. Pursue more.
Go higher and bang on heaven's door
to ask for answers that before
you wanted buried.

But of course, the choice is yours.
To swim in tepid waters on native shores,
to roam free in wilds unseen before.

To the person wondering if they are the only one

We are all as frail as glass
and maybe we should be as transparent
so we fully realize our own humanity
and leave behind our pride.

To the unsure one

sometimes fear talks louder than love.

To those who rise up

we don't accept rejection as an answer to these burdens
because You have heard us and You are unfazed.

To the old things I used to love

It's a twisted kind of irony
that these things which bring
life and light
can so easily be despised
or forgotten in the swirl of time.

To the one pursuing

Deep and shallow.
Shallow and deep.
Constant circles or dreamless sleep
reflect, ask, rest, seek.
This searching place does not come cheap.

Five

the healing

To the one who needs perspective

I am so small.
Fighting to be hopeful, water drop in a bucket of grace.
I am in this place solely because You decided that earth
should have a me, because You delight in making beauty
reality, here
 the grass is greener when I choose to be content.

I don't always choose to be content.
It is a peculiar sort of disease that makes
the eyes of a seeing person blind to everything that
conveniences them.
It is a belief that I am God and should be obeyed, it is
idol worship in its purest form-
self.
Aid me. I am holy, all-powerful, consuming and unwritten.
Remind me
remind me to be small.
Remind me that time is a measurement that I am held to and
it must be held wisely.
So many things on this earth are small and important and I,
I am one of these.

To the one holding onto worries

breathe in
shoulders tall
exhale
release it all   release it all
rise
        and
                    fall
rise
        and
                    fall
let the rhythm ease it all.
come for a second.
be held for a second.
release all the worries and hurries for a second.
breathe in again.
today, be free
it is over and
you can release.

To the one who notices small things

If the only thing that you do in this life
is appreciate beauty where it is hard to find
that is enough.
If all you do this week is relish in sunlight
that is enough.
Life is tough but
though you wonder when
you'll feel like you've made an impact again,
it is enough. You can be filled up.

Look at the colours complimenting each other.
Let that wash over you and fill you with wonder.
Tomorrow, when your words blunder and your world
thunders
stop
for a second
to remember the colours, the handiwork, the creativity
the things which others fail to see and
in doing this you're glorifying He who created.
This is enough.

To the person wondering why they are where they are

what if you believed
as in soul-searching, gut wrenching
chest h e a v i n g
belly calmed
kind of belief
that you are exactly where you are meant to be?

my friend, let me tell you
no one can fully lay down their roots
while they are constantly trying to move.

imagine
the colours that you would see
if you believed that this is where you're meant to be.
worry would cease
worry would cease
hunched shoulders would become children, free from unease
people become priorities, people to be loved and utterly
known.

fog consuming fields at dawn
burrows in the ground simply places to explore
people become treasures to be healed, not fixed, they
become
flowers to be cared for, tended to, weeds out and water down
and
patience, they will bloom when they are meant to.

when you are where you're supposed to be
people become treasures to be loved instead of objects to
please.
why try to fight a gentle breeze? you,
you are exactly where you're supposed to be.

To the overthinker

Let this season be one that heals
one that lets you see
the meadows dancing in the breeze or the way
the sunlight hits the trees.
Don't let worry be all that you feel.

To those who feel like they are constantly pushed back

Perhaps
when the weight of life burdens our lives
you will find that there is more than this reprise.
As you struggle bear in mind that you can still open your
eyes.
You are still alive.
Still you rise, guided by unseen hands to unknown lands
wading through the sands of the
everyday memories that you cannot discard.
It is hard.
And sometimes the sand stops you from going far
and it may seem as if you are thrust apart
from that which would relieve your struggle, but
consider this.

To struggle means you have not given in.
Still you rise.

To the one who needs peace

I'll create a place
where you can find peace.
No matter what's around
you can be at ease.
In Abba's arms, utter tranquility.

And on the days that you feel alone
and you cannot speak out and you want to go home
to see your father on his glorious throne
be still, be still, be still.

To the one worried about the future

Figure out life
piece by piece
stand back a while and let your worries cease
in the eye of the storm there is always some peace.

I know that the road you walk is unknown
and there are nights in the dark when it is yourself that you
loathe
and this path is untraveled and your hope is defused
by a landslide that's left you battered and bruised
and even now the trail has gone from your view-
these days are not ones you can fight your way through.

Rest. Find shade. Find ease in the burden that I have made.
Do not try to make sense of all this.
Do not try to be your own defense in all this.

Dear future self,
one day you'll see
God has put together the path
piece by piece.

To the one who worries about trusting others

Rest in your soul. Rest in your soul.
Do not let anxiety control.
Do not let fear stop you from being bold.
When the storms come and swirl your mind and you cannot
rest and you
cannot unwind
and you feel that you must strive and strive and strive
stop.
In the midst of your busy life
to breathe
to see
old things with new eyes or new things with acceptance.
Sometimes we reject them because we want the old things,
the comfortable things,
things we could depend on.
And when those things end,
we're unsure of whether anything will stay the same.

Inside of these foggy places full of days where you cannot
even recognize your own face,
learn that there is still grace.
There is still a place for you.
Even though valleys and pits abound,
you are always found. You always belong.

Holding on by yourself has made you strong and now
you are allowed
to let others in
to let anxiety out
to let go of the doubt that
you are wanted.

Value is not based on how you perform or how much you
fake or
how many blows you can take before you break.
You are worthy because He has claimed you for his own.
That is enough.
This is why heaven is home.
And tomorrow, when you try
to get it all right
and then crumble when you remember what you forgot last
night
rest your mind, rest your mind, rest your mind, rest your
mind.
It takes time but soon
this will all be fine.

To the one in-between

Embrace the calm-quiet-in-between
wonderfully whimsical lonely
space to breathe and unwind and find thoughts that you
thought had died,
heart urging for soul searching and questions that leave you
yearning to find more.

Before your world traps you in
find the place that your heart lives
decompress
look at the sky
and wonder and question and laugh and cry and
can you see the mountains?
Some are near,
some are far.
Some are so faded that it seems as if you dreamed them but
if you travel towards them
if you press on and crush in
and don't let tiredness win
don't let it win
you'll see you can make it to
them.

It is hard.
You'll want to cave.
You will rage and wonder why you didn't stay.
But if you choose to try it will pay.

When you wake up today there will be a thousand places and
people and schemes and dreams that you
crave but feel you cannot reach
don't give up.
They're only faded dreams
once you find them you will see
that since you waited
they are worth more than they could have been before the
journey
so let yourself release
all the pressure and unease
he sees, he sees, he sees, he sees
even when his promises are hard to believe.
Faith is simply a matter of
trusting that all he does is love
pursue him
he is there
and he's waiting for you
in the in between.

Author's Note

The idea that you can say anything and package it as a book and people will read it astounds me.

But here I am. I have joined those who scribble ideas and emotions, package them between two pieces of paper, and thrust them out into the world, hoping that it will touch someone's heart.

If Waiting Spaces has touched you, please consider leaving a review on GoodReads or Amazon. This gives me the chance to grow as an artist through your feedback and gives other people a greater chance of finding my work. I will read every piece of feedback I get! I look forwards to hearing how Waiting Spaces impacted you.

I am in the pursuit of glorifying God with what I have in whatever way I am able. My prayer is that Waiting Spaces has connected you to Him.

Keep searching,
Acacia Mitchell

Acknowledgements

Immense amounts of gratefulness are in order.
To Sophie Torrance, my fantastic friend and illustrator who took my poems and made art that brought tears to my eyes.

To my parents, who put in the time to encourage my writing and make it better.

To all of the friends who have given their time to help with design ideas, feedback, proofreading, or encouragement- you know who you are. It truly takes a village. Thank you all for everything.

Other places to find Acacia:

thoughtsfromatree.com
@acaciawritespoems
acaciawritespoetry@gmail.com

Printed in Great Britain
by Amazon